THE HAPPINESS PLANNER

focus on what makes you happy

belongs to

THE HAPPINESS PLANNER

focus on what makes you happy

It's been almost a year now since we launched The Happiness Planner. It makes me happy to know that the product we designed with love has made such a positive impact on people's lives. It has served the purpose we intended it to. Positive thinking is something that is so simple to grasp, yet, it may take years for us to successfully adopt the new mindset and attitude. Because we have been thinking, believing, and behaving a certain way for many years, we cannot simply have a paradigm shift in a short period of time. Just like any other muscle in our body, our brain needs to be trained in order to get stronger.

This is why we built The Happiness Planner - a tool designed to help you re-shape the way you think and to shift your focus to the positive. Because after all, what happens to you doesn't matter as much as how you perceive and react to what happens to you.

Beginning today, I'd like to encourage you to practice positive thinking and to build calmness and resilience in yourself in small ways. Often, it's the small daily setbacks that irritate us the most. We may feel as though the unfortunate events have stolen our happiness, when in fact, we take happiness away from ourselves when we are angry or upset. It is easy to get into a thought pattern of, "If things had turned out differently, I wouldn't be so upset." But when we use this type of thinking, we will likely find ourselves in more upsetting situations.

The key to long-lasting happiness is to learn not to become upset by small matters. When we learn to not sweat the small stuff - such as a delayed bus, bad weather, or a difficult colleague - eventually we will not sweat the big stuff. By doing this, we are not building our mind to become ignorant or permissive, but rather, to be able to withstand whatever comes our way. If we view problems as an opportunity to practice and grow, we will be blessed with the wisdoms of life and will feel a sense of inner peace and joy within ourselves.

Mo Seetubtim

Founder, Writer, Designer

Please connect with us

Instagram: @happinessplanner
Twitter: @happinessplannr
Facebook.com/happinessplanner
Facebook.com/groups/happinessplanner

For an extra dose of inspiration, sign up for our Happiness Email Series
http://www.bit.ly/DailyHappiness

Email: hello@thehappinessplanner.com

Please share your Happiness Planner photos
with us on Instagram and tag us.

10 Rules to live by for those who live a positive life.

1. Be comfortable in your own skin

2. Appreciate what you have and never compare yourself to others

3. See the positive in every situation

4. Let go of your need to control

5. Drop the resentment within

6. Live in the moment

7. Avoid overanalyzing

8. Stop worrying about the future

9. Drop your ego and be true

10. Have an open mind

"THE LONGER I LIVE, THE MORE I
REALIZE THE IMPACT OF ATTITUDE ON LIFE.
ATTITUDE, TO ME, IS MORE IMPORTANT THAN FACTS.
IT IS MORE IMPORTANT THAN THE PAST, THAN EDUCATION,
THAN MONEY, THAN CIRCUMSTANCES, THAN FAILURES,
THAN SUCCESSES, THAN WHAT OTHER PEOPLE THINK OR
SAY OR DO. IT IS MORE IMPORTANT THAN APPEARANCE,
GIFTEDNESS OR SKILL. IT WILL MAKE OR BREAK A COM-
PANY, A CHURCH, A HOME. THE REMARKABLE THING IS
WE HAVE A CHOICE EVERY DAY REGARDING THE ATTITUDE
WE WILL EMBRACE FOR THAT DAY. WE CANNOT CHANGE
OUR PAST. WE CANNOT CHANGE THE FACT THAT PEOPLE
WILL ACT IN A CERTAIN WAY. WE CANNOT CHANGE THE
INEVITABLE. THE ONLY THING WE CAN DO IS PLAY ON THE
ONE STRING WE HAVE, AND THAT IS OUR ATTITUDE. I AM
CONVINCED THAT LIFE IS 10% WHAT HAPPENS TO ME AND
90% HOW I REACT TO IT. AND SO IT IS WITH YOU.
WE ARE IN CHARGE OF OUR ATTITUDES."

- Charles R. Swindoll -

Create your

Happiness Roadmap

In this first section you will complete exercises that help you reflect on yourself. They are designed to get you to think about what makes you feel happy and fulfilled. The goal is to plan ahead for the next 100 days and to mindfully integrate happiness habits into your daily life.

Over the next 100 days, your focus and how you spend your time will be influenced by your answers in this first section.

The art of being happy lies in the power of extracting happiness from common things.

- Henry Ward Beecher -

1. WHAT MAKES YOU HAPPY ?

(1) Take a few minutes to think about the things in your life that bring you happiness. What do you do that makes you feel joy from within? What brings a smile to your face? What gives you energy and excitement? What are you passionate about? What gives your life meaning? It could be going to the beach, helping a stranger with directions, or traveling.

(2) Based on how happy each item or activity makes you feel, assign scores between 1 and 10. If it makes you extremely happy, give it a 10. If it makes you somewhat happy, give it a 5, and so on.

(3) Decide how often you will integrate these activities into your life. Perhaps it is something you will only do once, or you might choose to integrate these things on a daily, weekly, or monthly basis.

WHAT MAKES ME HAPPY	HOW GOOD DOES IT MAKE ME FEEL?	HOW OFTEN SHOULD I DO IT?
(Example) *Reading*	9	*daily*

Your life does not get better by chance, it gets better by change.

- Jim Rohn -

2. WHAT MAKES YOU UNHAPPY ?

(1) Look back at the past year and think about the times you felt unhappy, upset, angry, guilty, or bored. What made you unhappy? It could be your job, a negative friend, a bad habit that generates unpleasant consequences, a relationship with someone in your life, or an illness. In order to acknowledge the stressors or challenges in your life, make a list. This is the first step in making a conscious decision to remove them from your life.

(2) Based on how much it affects you, give each item a score between 1 and 10. Give it a 10 if it makes you extremely unhappy. Give it a 1 if it makes you only slightly unhappy.

(3) Assess whether you can change the situation or not. If so, how can you change it?

WHAT MAKES ME UNHAPPY	HOW MUCH DOES IT AFFECT ME?	CAN I CHANGE IT?	WHAT CAN I DO TO CHANGE THE SITUATION?
(Example) My job	8	(YES) NO	
		YES NO	
		YES NO	
		YES NO	
		YES NO	
		YES NO	
		YES NO	
		YES NO	
		YES NO	
		YES NO	
		YES NO	

3. WHAT ARE YOUR STRENGTHS ?

Identify your strengths by circling them below. Rank each trait by considering 1) how strongly you identify with each trait, and 2) the pride you feel for each trait.

Action-Oriented	Adventurous	Analytical	Artistic	Athletic
Authentic	Caring	Clever	Compassionate	Charming
Communicative	Confident	Courageous	Creative	Curious
Determined	Disciplined	Educated	Empathetic	Emotional
Energetic	Entertaining	Fast	Flexible	Focused
Helping	Inspiring	Intelligent	Leadership	Learning
Motivated	Optimistic	Open-Minded	Organized	Outgoing
Patient	Precise	Responsible	Self-Controlled	Speaking
Spontaneous	Social Skills	Strategic Thinking	Team-Oriented	Thoughtful
Trustworthy	Visionary	Warm	Willpower	Wisdom

1 ....   4 ....

2 ....   5 ....

3 ....   6 ....

> **WHEN WE'RE ABLE TO PUT MOST OF OUR ENERGY INTO DEVELOPING OUR NATURAL TALENTS, EXTRAORDINARY ROOM FOR GROWTH EXISTS. THE KEY TO HUMAN DEVELOPMENT IS BUILDING ON WHO YOU ALREADY ARE.**
>
> - Tom Rath -

4. WHAT ARE YOUR WEAKNESSES ?

Identify your weaknesses by circling them below. Rank each trait by considering 1) how strongly you identify with each trait, and 2) how disastisfied or annoyed you are with each trait.

Weaknesses are natural - we all have them. But in order to improve ourselves, we need to identify our weakness. This allows us to work through them and push ourselves to grow.

Aggressive	Arrogant	Bossy	Chaotic	Close-minded
Complaining	Contemptuous	Controlling	Cynical	Fearful
Greedy	Hesitant	Ignorant	Impatient	Impulsive
Indifferent	Insensitive	Intolerant	Irresponsible	Lazy
Lethargic	Loose-tongued	Mistrustful	Moody	Naive
Negative	Obstructive	Passive	Prejudiced	Reckless
Rude	Selfish	Shallow	Short-sighted	Shy
Sloppy	Stubborn	Slow	Strict	Undisciplined
Vague	Wasteful			

1 ....

2 ....

3 ....

4 ....

5 ....

6 ....

EVERYONE IS A GENIUS. BUT IF YOU JUDGE A FISH ON ITS ABILITY TO CLIMB A TREE, IT WILL LIVE ITS WHOLE LIFE BELIEVING THAT IT IS STUPID.

- Albert Einstein -

Patience is a key that unlocks the door to a more fulfilling life. it is through a cultivation of patience that we become better parents, powerful teachers, great business-men, good friends, and live a happier life.

- Steve Maraboli -

5. WHAT DO YOU NORMALLY GET UPSET OR FRUSTRATED ABOUT?

Think about the times that you become upset or frustrated. Your frustration could be caused by a small daily inconvenience or a larger challenge. What do you normally get upset about? What irritates you? What makes you frustrated? Do you normally become frustrated when your house is untidy? Do you get upset when the train is delayed? Are you easily annoyed by a certain colleague? Do you find yourself in a bad mood during a traffic jam?

Identifying the source of your frustration can help you realize how small some of them truly are. By being aware of the scale of your frustrations, you can learn to monitor your thoughts and emotions and consciously train yourself to be more accepting and understanding of matters that are outside of your control. Repeating this exercise, beginning with the smallest irritations, will help you become the master of your own mind and feel more control over your life.

WHAT FRUSRTATES ME	IS IT BEYOND MY CONTROL?	IF NO, WHAT CAN I DO TO MAKE THE SITUATION BETTER?
(Example) Traffic	(YES) NO	
	YES NO	
	YES NO	
	YES NO	
	YES NO	
	YES NO	
	YES NO	
	YES NO	
	YES NO	
	YES NO	

The habits that took years to build, do not take a day to change.

- Susan Powter -

6. WHAT QUALITIES OR HABITS WOULD YOU LIKE TO IMPROVE ?

Write down the qualities and habits that you would like to improve or change. Then spend some time thinking about how you would like to improve them. Integrate these concrete steps into your schedule in order to begin manifesting change.

Examples of inner qualities include cleanliness, calmness, positivity, or self-confidence. Examples of habits include quitting smoking or drinking.

WHAT I'D LIKE TO IMPROVE ON	HOW
(Example) Cleaner	Always clean up after myself
(Example) Calmer	Learn to control my temper

7. WHAT AND WHO ARE YOU GRATEFUL FOR IN YOUR LIFE ?

Gratitude is a powerful way of thinking that can greatly increase your happiness level. When you practice gratitude, you are reminded of the positive people, activities, and items that you have in your life. A gratitude practice also helps you recognize the beauty around you and serves as a reminder to appreciate the small things in life.

We are all inherently blessed in certain ways - be it a natural ability or specific opportunities we have been afforded. Moreover, we all have special people who have shaped our lives for the better. Our lives would be very different without these people.

Make a conscious acknowledgement of this and express your gratitude for the people who have helped you in some way.

(Example) *My supportive family*

8. WHO WOULD YOU LIKE TO SEE MORE OFTEN ?

In our busy world, it is easy to become caught up in work and other responsibilities. We might forget to set aside time for the people we love and care about. It is important to remember that at the end of the day, it is our relationships that make life worthlife.

Write down the names of the people you would like to see more often over the next 100 days. Think about how you would like to spend time with them, and write that down as well.

WHO I'D LIKE TO SEE MORE OFTEN	THINGS TO DO TOGETHER
(Example) *Mom*	*Take her shopping*

9. WHAT HAVE YOU ACHIEVED SO FAR THAT YOU'RE PROUD OF ?

Write down all of the wonderful things you've done in your life. Your list might include specific achievements, growthful experiences, places you've been, and people you've met.

This list is to remind you of the proud and happy moments you've experienced so that you can feel inspired and excited for the future.

10. WHAT ARE YOUR DREAMS ? WHAT DO YOU WANT TO ACHIEVE IN LIFE ?

It is often said that you should "follow your dreams". Our dreams inspire us, give us hope, and instill the drive to move forward. Without dreams, we lack tangible goals and aspirations.

We all want different things in life. Writing down your dreams can provide motivation and keep you focused on your goals. What are your dreams? What activities or accomplishments would you include on your bucketlist? What experiences will you regret not having should you not achieve them in your lifetime?

Ten years from now,
make sure you can say
that you chose your life,
you didn't settle for it.

- Mandy Hale -

11. HOW DO YOU SEE YOURSELF IN 5-10 YEARS ?

PERSONALLY	PROFESSIONALLY	
		5 years
		10 years

What you get by achieving your goals is not as important as what you become by achieving your goals.

- Zig Ziglar -

12. WHAT DO YOU WANT TO ACHIEVE IN 100 DAYS?

When our lives change, our priorities also change. The goals we created a year ago may be completely different from the goals we are setting today. Some of us may have achieved the goals we set for ourselves, while others may have entered a new stage of life and adopted new goals instead. It is important to periodically review our life plans. Even if you are a naturally spontaneous person, you will benefit from having goals to stay focused.

Write down what you want to achieve in the span of 100 days. Start with the big picture and work all the way down to the small steps you will need to achieve your goals.

Life has its own pace.
You can have it all,
just not all at once.
And if you don't keep
your focus right,
you might not
achieve anything.

- Mo Seetubtim -

SUM UP WHAT YOU WANT TO ACHIEVE OVER THE NEXT 100 DAYS

After evaluating all of the factors that make up your life and contribute to your happiness level, the next step is to set goals. When you make plans to integrate more of what makes you happy into your life, you are also able to identify and change what holds you back. This process helps you to work towards self-improvement and being the best person you can be.

In this section, sum up the key things you will do and achieve over the next 100 days. This could be a self-improvement goal (i.e. being more positive and mindful), a habit change (i.e. quitting smoking), or a work goal (i.e. launching your business in another market).

Make sure you focus on one thing at a time.

2016

JANUARY

M	T	W	T	F	S	S
				1	2	3
4	5	6	7	8	9	10
11	12	13	14	15	16	17
18	19	20	21	22	23	24
25	26	27	28	29	30	31

FEBRUARY

M	T	W	T	F	S	S
1	2	3	4	5	6	7
8	9	10	11	12	13	14
15	16	17	18	19	20	21
22	23	24	25	26	27	28
29						

MARCH

M	T	W	T	F	S	S
	1	2	3	4	5	6
7	8	9	10	11	12	13
14	15	16	17	18	19	20
21	22	23	24	25	26	27
28	29	30	31			

APRIL

M	T	W	T	F	S	S
				1	2	3
4	5	6	7	8	9	10
11	12	13	14	15	16	17
18	19	20	21	22	23	24
25	26	27	28	29	30	

MAY

M	T	W	T	F	S	S
						1
2	3	4	5	6	7	8
9	10	11	12	13	14	15
16	17	18	19	20	21	22
23	24	25	26	27	28	29
30	31					

JUNE

M	T	W	T	F	S	S
		1	2	3	4	5
6	7	8	9	10	11	12
13	14	15	16	17	18	19
20	21	22	23	24	25	26
27	28	29	30			

JULY

M	T	W	T	F	S	S
				1	2	3
4	5	6	7	8	9	10
11	12	13	14	15	16	17
18	19	20	21	22	23	24
25	26	27	28	29	30	31

AUGUST

M	T	W	T	F	S	S
1	2	3	4	5	6	7
8	9	10	11	12	13	14
15	16	17	18	19	20	21
22	23	24	25	26	27	28
29	30	31				

SEPTEMBER

M	T	W	T	F	S	S
			1	2	3	4
5	6	7	8	9	10	11
12	13	14	15	16	17	18
19	20	21	22	23	24	25
26	27	28	29	30		

OCTOBER

M	T	W	T	F	S	S
					1	2
3	4	5	6	7	8	9
10	11	12	13	14	15	16
17	18	19	20	21	22	23
24	25	26	27	28	29	30
31						

NOVEMBER

M	T	W	T	F	S	S
	1	2	3	4	5	6
7	8	9	10	11	12	13
14	15	16	17	18	19	20
21	22	23	24	25	26	27
28	29	30				

DECEMBER

M	T	W	T	F	S	S
			1	2	3	4
5	6	7	8	9	10	11
12	13	14	15	16	17	18
19	20	21	22	23	24	25
26	27	28	29	30	31	

2017

JANUARY

M	T	W	T	F	S	S
						1
2	3	4	5	6	7	8
9	10	11	12	13	14	15
16	17	18	19	20	21	22
23	24	25	26	27	28	29
30	31					

FEBRUARY

M	T	W	T	F	S	S
		1	2	3	4	5
6	7	8	9	10	11	12
13	14	15	16	17	18	19
20	21	22	23	24	25	26
27	28					

MARCH

M	T	W	T	F	S	S
		1	2	3	4	5
6	7	8	9	10	11	12
13	14	15	16	17	18	19
20	21	22	23	24	25	26
27	28	29	30	31		

APRIL

M	T	W	T	F	S	S
					1	2
3	4	5	6	7	8	9
10	11	12	13	14	15	16
17	18	19	20	21	22	23
24	25	26	27	28	29	30

MAY

M	T	W	T	F	S	S
1	2	3	4	5	6	7
8	9	10	11	12	13	14
15	16	17	18	19	20	21
22	23	24	25	26	27	28
29	30	31				

JUNE

M	T	W	T	F	S	S
			1	2	3	4
5	6	7	8	9	10	11
12	13	14	15	16	17	18
19	20	21	22	23	24	25
26	27	28	29	30		

JULY

M	T	W	T	F	S	S
					1	2
3	4	5	6	7	8	9
10	11	12	13	14	15	16
17	18	19	20	21	22	23
24	25	26	27	28	29	30
31						

AUGUST

M	T	W	T	F	S	S
	1	2	3	4	5	6
7	8	9	10	11	12	13
14	15	16	17	18	19	20
21	22	23	24	25	26	27
28	29	30	31			

SEPTEMBER

M	T	W	T	F	S	S
				1	2	3
4	5	6	7	8	9	10
11	12	13	14	15	16	17
18	19	20	21	22	23	24
25	26	27	28	29	30	

OCTOBER

M	T	W	T	F	S	S
						1
2	3	4	5	6	7	8
9	10	11	12	13	14	15
16	17	18	19	20	21	22
23	24	25	26	27	28	29
30	31					

NOVEMBER

M	T	W	T	F	S	S
		1	2	3	4	5
6	7	8	9	10	11	12
13	14	15	16	17	18	19
20	21	22	23	24	25	26
27	28	29	30			

DECEMBER

M	T	W	T	F	S	S
				1	2	3
4	5	6	7	8	9	10
11	12	13	14	15	16	17
18	19	20	21	22	23	24
25	26	27	28	29	30	31

Before you get started, please rate how you feel.

Unhappy	1	2	3	4	5	Happy
Bored	1	2	3	4	5	Excited
Tired	1	2	3	4	5	Energetic
Stressed	1	2	3	4	5	Calm
Unhealthy	1	2	3	4	5	Healthy

100 Days

of happiness, positivity, mindfulness, gratitude, and self-development.

WEEKLY PLAN

MONDAY :

TUESDAY :

WEDNESDAY :

THURSDAY :

FRIDAY :

SATURDAY :

SUNDAY :

NOTES :

DAY 1

"The best investment you'll ever make is in yourself. Never stop exploring, learning, experiencing, and becoming a better person every day."

- Mo Seetubtim -

TODAY I'M EXCITED ABOUT :

EXERCISES :

MAIN FOCUS :

MEALS :

SCHEDULE :

TO-DOS :

- [ ]
- [ ]
- [ ]
- [ ]
- [ ]
- [ ]

NOTES :

GOOD THINGS ABOUT TODAY :

WHAT I HOPE FOR TOMORROW :

DAY 2

"The key question to keep asking is, are you spending your time on the right things?
Because time is all you have."
- Randy Pausch -

TODAY I'M EXCITED ABOUT :

EXERCISES :

MAIN FOCUS :

MEALS :

SCHEDULE :

TO-DOS :

- [ ]
- [ ]
- [ ]
- [ ]
- [ ]
- [ ]

NOTES :

GOOD THINGS ABOUT TODAY :

WHAT I HOPE FOR TOMORROW :

DAY 3

"Challenges are what make life interesting; overcoming them is what makes life meaningful."
- Joshua J. Marine

TODAY I'M EXCITED ABOUT :

EXERCISES :

MAIN FOCUS :

MEALS :

SCHEDULE :

TO-DOS :

- [ ]
- [ ]
- [ ]
- [ ]
- [ ]
- [ ]

NOTES :

GOOD THINGS ABOUT TODAY :

WHAT I HOPE FOR TOMORROW :

DAY 4

"Whatever thoughts are causing you pain, they are only thoughts. You can change a thought."
- Andrew Matthews -

TODAY I'M EXCITED ABOUT :

EXERCISES :

MAIN FOCUS :

MEALS :

SCHEDULE :

TO-DOS :

- [ ]
- [ ]
- [ ]
- [ ]
- [ ]
- [ ]

NOTES :

GOOD THINGS ABOUT TODAY :

WHAT I HOPE FOR TOMORROW :

DAY 5

"Patience can't be acquired overnight. It is just like building up a muscle.
Every day you need to work on it."
- Eknath Easwaran -

TODAY I'M EXCITED ABOUT :

EXERCISES :

MAIN FOCUS :

MEALS :

SCHEDULE :

TO-DOS :

- [ ]
- [ ]
- [ ]
- [ ]
- [ ]
- [ ]

NOTES :

GOOD THINGS ABOUT TODAY :

WHAT I HOPE FOR TOMORROW :

DAY 6

"The best thing to do when you find yourself in a hurting or vulnerable place is to surround yourself with the strongest, finest, most positive people you know."
- Kristin Armstrong -

TODAY I'M EXCITED ABOUT :

EXERCISES :

MAIN FOCUS :

MEALS :

SCHEDULE :

TO-DOS :

- [ ]
- [ ]
- [ ]
- [ ]
- [ ]
- [ ]

NOTES :

GOOD THINGS ABOUT TODAY :

WHAT I HOPE FOR TOMORROW :

DAY 7

"It is better to conquer yourself than to win a thousand battles. Then the victory is yours.
It cannot be taken from you, not by angels or by demons, heaven or hell."
- Buddha -

TODAY I'M EXCITED ABOUT :

EXERCISES :

MAIN FOCUS :

MEALS :

SCHEDULE :

TO-DOS :

- [ ]
- [ ]
- [ ]
- [ ]
- [ ]
- [ ]

NOTES :

GOOD THINGS ABOUT TODAY :

WHAT I HOPE FOR TOMORROW :

WEEKLY REFLECTION

DESCRIBE THIS PAST WEEK IN 3 WORDS :

Unhappy	1	2	3	4	5	Happy
Bored	1	2	3	4	5	Excited
Tired	1	2	3	4	5	Energetic
Stressed	1	2	3	4	5	Calm
Unhealthy	1	2	3	4	5	Healthy

Score _____ / 25

THIS WEEK'S HIGHS - GOOD / HAPPY / PROUD MOMENTS

THIS WEEK'S LOWS - FRUSTRATIONS / CHALLENGES / STRUGGLES

WEEKLY REFLECTION

WHAT I LEARNED THIS WEEK :

WHO & WHAT I'M THANKFUL FOR :

WHAT I'D LIKE TO IMPROVE / WHAT I HOPE FOR :

WEEKLY PLAN

MONDAY :

TUESDAY :

WEDNESDAY :

THURSDAY :

FRIDAY :

SATURDAY :

SUNDAY :

NOTES :

/
DATE

DAY 8

"The pain you feel today will be the strength you feel tomorrow.
There is no easy way to any place worth going."
- Unknown -

TODAY I'M EXCITED ABOUT :

EXERCISES :

MAIN FOCUS :

MEALS :

SCHEDULE :

TO-DOS :

- [ ]
- [ ]
- [ ]
- [ ]
- [ ]
- [ ]

NOTES :

GOOD THINGS ABOUT TODAY :

WHAT I HOPE FOR TOMORROW :

DATE /

DAY 9

"Give the one you love wings to fly, roots to come back, and reasons to stay."
- Dalai Lama -

TODAY I'M EXCITED ABOUT :

EXERCISES :

MAIN FOCUS :

MEALS :

SCHEDULE :

TO-DOS :

- [ ]
- [ ]
- [ ]
- [ ]
- [ ]
- [ ]

NOTES :

GOOD THINGS ABOUT TODAY :

WHAT I HOPE FOR TOMORROW :

DAY 10

"The walls we build around us to keep sadness out also keeps out the joy."
- Jim Rohn -

TODAY I'M EXCITED ABOUT :

EXERCISES :

MAIN FOCUS :

MEALS :

SCHEDULE :

TO-DOS :

- [ ]
- [ ]
- [ ]
- [ ]
- [ ]
- [ ]

NOTES :

GOOD THINGS ABOUT TODAY :

WHAT I HOPE FOR TOMORROW :

DAY 11

"There is only one way to happiness and that is to cease worrying about things which are beyond the power of our will."
- Epictetus

TODAY I'M EXCITED ABOUT :

EXERCISES :

MAIN FOCUS :

MEALS :

SCHEDULE :

TO-DOS :

- [ ]
- [ ]
- [ ]
- [ ]
- [ ]
- [ ]

NOTES :

GOOD THINGS ABOUT TODAY :

WHAT I HOPE FOR TOMORROW :

DAY 12

"The minute you stop improving yourself is the minute your life becomes stale.
Never stop challenging yourself to become the best you can be."
- Mo Seetubtim -

TODAY I'M EXCITED ABOUT :

EXERCISES :

MAIN FOCUS :

MEALS :

SCHEDULE :

TO-DOS :

- [ ]
- [ ]
- [ ]
- [ ]
- [ ]
- [ ]

NOTES :

GOOD THINGS ABOUT TODAY :

WHAT I HOPE FOR TOMORROW :

DAY 13

"Don't gain the world and lose your soul. Wisdom is better than silver or gold."
- Bob Marley -

TODAY I'M EXCITED ABOUT :

EXERCISES :

MAIN FOCUS :

MEALS :

SCHEDULE :

TO-DOS :

- [ ]
- [ ]
- [ ]
- [ ]
- [ ]
- [ ]

NOTES :

GOOD THINGS ABOUT TODAY :

WHAT I HOPE FOR TOMORROW :

DAY 14

"Don't ask yourself what the world needs. Ask yourself what makes you come alive and
go do that, because what the world needs is people who have come alive."
- Howard Thurman -

TODAY I'M EXCITED ABOUT :

EXERCISES :

MAIN FOCUS :

MEALS :

SCHEDULE :

TO-DOS :

- [ ]
- [ ]
- [ ]
- [ ]
- [ ]
- [ ]

NOTES :

GOOD THINGS ABOUT TODAY :

WHAT I HOPE FOR TOMORROW :

WEEKLY REFLECTION

DESCRIBE THIS PAST WEEK IN 3 WORDS :

	1	2	3	4	5	
Unhappy	1	2	3	4	5	Happy
Borod	1	2	3	4	5	Excited
Tired	1	2	3	4	5	Energetic
Stressed	1	2	3	4	5	Calm
Unhealthy	1	2	3	4	5	Healthy

Score _____ / 25

THIS WEEK'S HIGHS - GOOD / HAPPY / PROUD MOMENTS

THIS WEEK'S LOWS - FRUSTRATIONS / CHALLENGES / STRUGGLES

WEEKLY REFLECTION

WHAT I LEARNED THIS WEEK :

WHO & WHAT I'M THANKFUL FOR :

WHAT I'D LIKE TO IMPROVE / WHAT I HOPE FOR :

WEEKLY PLAN

MONDAY :

TUESDAY :

WEDNESDAY :

THURSDAY :

FRIDAY :

SATURDAY :

SUNDAY :

NOTES :

DAY 15

"The first step to happiness is to stop complaining. When you complain, not only do you fill yourself up with negativity, but you also spread the negative energy to those around you. Complaining makes you feel even worse and become an unpleasant person to be around. Break the habit today!"

TODAY I'M EXCITED ABOUT :

EXERCISES :

MAIN FOCUS :

MEALS :

SCHEDULE :

TO-DOS :

- [ ]
- [ ]
- [ ]
- [ ]
- [ ]
- [ ]

NOTES :

GOOD THINGS ABOUT TODAY :

WHAT I HOPE FOR TOMORROW :

DAY 16

"Our ambition should be to rule ourselves, the true kingdom for each one of us;
and true progress is to know more, and be more, and to do more."
- Oscar Wilde -

TODAY I'M EXCITED ABOUT :

EXERCISES :

MAIN FOCUS :

MEALS :

SCHEDULE :

TO-DOS :

- [ ]
- [ ]
- [ ]
- [ ]
- [ ]
- [ ]

NOTES :

GOOD THINGS ABOUT TODAY :

WHAT I HOPE FOR TOMORROW :

DAY 17

Pick who you hang around with wisely. The energy from those around you has
a serious effect on how you feel about life and the world."
- Mo Seetubtim -

TODAY I'M EXCITED ABOUT :

EXERCISES :

MAIN FOCUS :

MEALS :

SCHEDULE :

TO-DOS :

- [ ]
- [ ]
- [ ]
- [ ]
- [ ]
- [ ]

NOTES :

GOOD THINGS ABOUT TODAY :

WHAT I HOPE FOR TOMORROW :

DAY 18

"Research has shown that best way to be happy is to make each day happy."
- Deepak Chopra -

TODAY I'M EXCITED ABOUT :

EXERCISES :

MAIN FOCUS :

MEALS :

SCHEDULE :

TO-DOS :

- [ ]
- [ ]
- [ ]
- [ ]
- [ ]
- [ ]

NOTES :

GOOD THINGS ABOUT TODAY :

WHAT I HOPE FOR TOMORROW :

DAY 19

"What holds most people back isn't the quality of their ideas, but their lack of faith in themselves.
You have to live your life as if you are already where you want to be."
- Russell Simmons -

TODAY I'M EXCITED ABOUT :

EXERCISES :

MAIN FOCUS :

MEALS :

SCHEDULE :

TO-DOS :

☐

☐

☐

☐

☐

☐

NOTES :

GOOD THINGS ABOUT TODAY :

WHAT I HOPE FOR TOMORROW :

DAY 20

"The joy of life comes from our encounters with new experiences, and hence there is no greater joy than to have an endlessly changing horizon, for each day to have a new and different sun."
- Christopher McCandless -

TODAY I'M EXCITED ABOUT :

EXERCISES :

MAIN FOCUS :

MEALS :

SCHEDULE :

TO-DOS :

☐

☐

☐

☐

☐

☐

NOTES :

GOOD THINGS ABOUT TODAY :

WHAT I HOPE FOR TOMORROW :

DAY 21

"Be a reflection of what you'd like to see in others. If you want love give love. If you want honesty,
give honesty. If you want respect, give respect. You get in return what you give."
- Unknown -

TODAY I'M EXCITED ABOUT :

EXERCISES :

MAIN FOCUS :

MEALS :

SCHEDULE :

TO-DOS :

- [ ]
- [ ]
- [ ]
- [ ]
- [ ]
- [ ]

NOTES :

GOOD THINGS ABOUT TODAY :

WHAT I HOPE FOR TOMORROW :

WEEKLY REFLECTION

DESCRIBE THIS PAST WEEK IN 3 WORDS :

Unhappy	1	2	3	4	5	Happy
Bored	1	2	3	4	5	Excited
Tired	1	2	3	4	5	Energetic
Stressed	1	2	3	4	5	Calm
Unhealthy	1	2	3	4	5	Healthy

Score _____ / 25

THIS WEEK'S HIGHS - GOOD / HAPPY / PROUD MOMENTS

THIS WEEK'S LOWS - FRUSTRATIONS / CHALLENGES / STRUGGLES

WHAT I LEARNED THIS WEEK :

WHO & WHAT I'M THANKFUL FOR :

WHAT I'D LIKE TO IMPROVE / WHAT I HOPE FOR :

WEEKLY PLAN

MONDAY :

TUESDAY :

WEDNESDAY :

THURSDAY :

FRIDAY :

SATURDAY :

SUNDAY :

NOTES :

DAY 22

"Surround yourself with the dreamers and doers, the believers and thinkers, but most of all, surround yourself with those who see the greatness within you, even when you don't see it yourself."
- Edmund Lee-

TODAY I'M EXCITED ABOUT :

EXERCISES :

MAIN FOCUS :

MEALS :

SCHEDULE :

TO-DOS :

- [ ]
- [ ]
- [ ]
- [ ]
- [ ]
- [ ]

NOTES :

GOOD THINGS ABOUT TODAY :

WHAT I HOPE FOR TOMORROW :

DAY 23

"Before you find your soul mate, you must first discover your soul."
- Charles F. Glassman -

TODAY I'M EXCITED ABOUT :

EXERCISES :

MAIN FOCUS :

MEALS :

SCHEDULE :

TO-DOS :

☐

☐

☐

☐

☐

☐

NOTES :

GOOD THINGS ABOUT TODAY :

WHAT I HOPE FOR TOMORROW :

DAY 24

"Time does not heal everything but acceptance will heal everything."
- Buddha -

TODAY I'M EXCITED ABOUT :

EXERCISES :

MAIN FOCUS :

MEALS :

SCHEDULE :

TO-DOS :

- [ ]
- [ ]
- [ ]
- [ ]
- [ ]
- [ ]

NOTES :

GOOD THINGS ABOUT TODAY :

WHAT I HOPE FOR TOMORROW :

DAY 25

"A bird sitting on a tree is never afraid of the branch breaking, because her trust is not on the branch but on her own wings. Always believe in yourself."
- Unknown -

TODAY I'M EXCITED ABOUT :

EXERCISES :

MAIN FOCUS :

MEALS :

SCHEDULE :

TO-DOS :

☐

☐

☐

☐

☐

☐

NOTES :

GOOD THINGS ABOUT TODAY :

WHAT I HOPE FOR TOMORROW :

DAY 26

"You can never cross the ocean until you have the courage to lose sight of the shore."
- Christopher Columbus -

TODAY I'M EXCITED ABOUT :

EXERCISES :

MAIN FOCUS :

MEALS :

SCHEDULE :

TO-DOS :

- [ ]
- [ ]
- [ ]
- [ ]
- [ ]
- [ ]

NOTES :

GOOD THINGS ABOUT TODAY :

WHAT I HOPE FOR TOMORROW :

DAY 27

"The people you surround yourself with influence your behaviors, so choose
friends who have healthy habits."
- Dan Buettner -

TODAY I'M EXCITED ABOUT :

EXERCISES :

MAIN FOCUS :

MEALS :

SCHEDULE :

TO-DOS :

☐

☐

☐

☐

☐

☐

NOTES :

GOOD THINGS ABOUT TODAY :

WHAT I HOPE FOR TOMORROW :

DATE

DAY 28

"In life, the things that go wrong are often the very things that lead to other things going right."
- Arianna Huffington -

TODAY I'M EXCITED ABOUT :

EXERCISES :

MAIN FOCUS :

MEALS :

SCHEDULE :

TO-DOS :

☐
☐
☐
☐
☐
☐

NOTES :

GOOD THINGS ABOUT TODAY :

WHAT I HOPE FOR TOMORROW :

WEEKLY REFLECTION

DESCRIBE THIS PAST WEEK IN 3 WORDS :

Unhappy	1	2	3	4	5	Happy
Bored	1	2	3	4	5	Excited
Tired	1	2	3	4	5	Energetic
Stressed	1	2	3	4	5	Calm
Unhealthy	1	2	3	4	5	Healthy

Score _____ / 25

THIS WEEK'S HIGHS - GOOD / HAPPY / PROUD MOMENTS

THIS WEEK'S LOWS - FRUSTRATIONS / CHALLENGES / STRUGGLES

WEEKLY REFLECTION

WHAT I LEARNED THIS WEEK :

WHO & WHAT I'M THANKFUL FOR :

WHAT I'D LIKE TO IMPROVE / WHAT I HOPE FOR :

WEEKLY PLAN

MONDAY :

TUESDAY :

WEDNESDAY :

THURSDAY :

FRIDAY :

SATURDAY :

SUNDAY :

NOTES :

DAY 29

"For what it's worth: it's never too late to be whoever you want to be. I hope you live a life you're proud of, and if you find you're not, I hope you have the strength to start over again."
- F. Scott Fitzgerald -

TODAY I'M EXCITED ABOUT :

EXERCISES :

MAIN FOCUS :

MEALS :

SCHEDULE :

TO-DOS :

☐

☐

☐

☐

☐

☐

NOTES :

GOOD THINGS ABOUT TODAY :

WHAT I HOPE FOR TOMORROW :

DAY 30

"You cannot control what happens to you, but you can control your attitude toward what happens to you, and in that, you will be mastering change rather than allowing it to master you."
- Brian Tracy -

TODAY I'M EXCITED ABOUT :

EXERCISES :

MAIN FOCUS :

MEALS :

SCHEDULE :

TO-DOS :

- [ ]
- [ ]
- [ ]
- [ ]
- [ ]
- [ ]

NOTES :

GOOD THINGS ABOUT TODAY :

WHAT I HOPE FOR TOMORROW :

DAY 31

"If you don't go after what you want, you'll never have it. If you don't ask, the
answer is always no. If you don't step forward, you're always in the same place."
- Nora Roberts -

TODAY I'M EXCITED ABOUT :

EXERCISES :

MAIN FOCUS :

MEALS :

SCHEDULE :

TO-DOS :

- [ ]
- [ ]
- [ ]
- [ ]
- [ ]
- [ ]

NOTES :

GOOD THINGS ABOUT TODAY :

WHAT I HOPE FOR TOMORROW :

DAY 32

"The three components of happiness are; something to do, something to love,
and something to look forward to."
- Dr. Gordon Livingston -

TODAY I'M EXCITED ABOUT :

EXERCISES :

MAIN FOCUS :

MEALS :

SCHEDULE :

TO-DOS :

- [ ]
- [ ]
- [ ]
- [ ]
- [ ]
- [ ]

NOTES :

GOOD THINGS ABOUT TODAY :

WHAT I HOPE FOR TOMORROW :

DATE

DAY 33

"Be at war with your vices, at peace with your neighbors, at ease with your inner self,
and let every new year find you a better person."

TODAY I'M EXCITED ABOUT :

EXERCISES :

MAIN FOCUS :

MEALS :

SCHEDULE :

TO-DOS :

- [ ]
- [ ]
- [ ]
- [ ]
- [ ]
- [ ]

NOTES :

GOOD THINGS ABOUT TODAY :

WHAT I HOPE FOR TOMORROW :

/
DATE

DAY 34

"To all the other dreamers out there, don't ever stop or let the world's negativity disenchant you
or your spirit. If you surround yourself with love and the right people, anything is possible."
- Adam Green -

TODAY I'M EXCITED ABOUT :

EXERCISES :

MAIN FOCUS :

MEALS :

SCHEDULE :

TO-DOS :

- [ ]
- [ ]
- [ ]
- [ ]
- [ ]
- [ ]

NOTES :

GOOD THINGS ABOUT TODAY :

WHAT I HOPE FOR TOMORROW :

DAY 35

"If you reduce your happiness box from one big one to many little ones,
then you can fill it up every day."
- Mo Seetubtim -

TODAY I'M EXCITED ABOUT :

EXERCISES :

MAIN FOCUS :

MEALS :

SCHEDULE :

TO-DOS :

☐

☐

☐

☐

☐

☐

NOTES :

GOOD THINGS ABOUT TODAY :

WHAT I HOPE FOR TOMORROW :

WEEKLY REFLECTION

DESCRIBE THIS PAST WEEK IN 3 WORDS :

	1	2	3	4	5	
Unhappy	1	2	3	4	5	Happy
Bored	1	2	3	4	5	Excited
Tired	1	2	3	4	5	Energetic
Stressed	1	2	3	4	5	Calm
Unhealthy	1	2	3	4	5	Healthy

Score _____ / 25

THIS WEEK'S HIGHS - GOOD / HAPPY / PROUD MOMENTS

THIS WEEK'S LOWS - FRUSTRATIONS / CHALLENGES / STRUGGLES

WEEKLY REFLECTION

WHAT I LEARNED THIS WEEK :

WHO & WHAT I'M THANKFUL FOR :

WHAT I'D LIKE TO IMPROVE / WHAT I HOPE FOR :

WEEKLY PLAN

MONDAY :

TUESDAY :

WEDNESDAY :

THURSDAY :

FRIDAY :

SATURDAY :

SUNDAY :

NOTES :

DAY 36

"To heal a wound you need to stop touching it."
- Unknown -

TODAY I'M EXCITED ABOUT :

EXERCISES :

MAIN FOCUS :

MEALS :

SCHEDULE :

TO-DOS :

- [ ]
- [ ]
- [ ]
- [ ]
- [ ]
- [ ]

NOTES :

GOOD THINGS ABOUT TODAY :

WHAT I HOPE FOR TOMORROW :

DAY 37

"Don't become too pre-occupied with what is happening around you.
Pay more attention to what is going on within you."
- Buddha -

TODAY I'M EXCITED ABOUT :

EXERCISES :

MAIN FOCUS :

MEALS :

SCHEDULE :

TO-DOS :

☐

☐

☐

☐

☐

☐

NOTES :

GOOD THINGS ABOUT TODAY :

WHAT I HOPE FOR TOMORROW :

/
DATE

DAY 38

"The greatest discovery of all time is that a person can change his future
by merely changing his attitude."
- Oprah Winfrey -

TODAY I'M EXCITED ABOUT :

EXERCISES :

MAIN FOCUS :

MEALS :

SCHEDULE :

TO-DOS :

- [ ]
- [ ]
- [ ]
- [ ]
- [ ]
- [ ]

NOTES :

GOOD THINGS ABOUT TODAY :

WHAT I HOPE FOR TOMORROW :

DAY 39

"Dream more of becoming than of obtaining."
- Unknown -

TODAY I'M EXCITED ABOUT :

EXERCISES :

MAIN FOCUS :

MEALS :

SCHEDULE :

TO-DOS :

- [ ]
- [ ]
- [ ]
- [ ]
- [ ]
- [ ]

NOTES :

GOOD THINGS ABOUT TODAY :

WHAT I HOPE FOR TOMORROW :

DAY 40

"Your ambition should be to get as much life out of living as you possibly can, as much enjoyment, as much interest, as much experience, and as much understanding."
- Eleanor Roosevelt -

TODAY I'M EXCITED ABOUT :

EXERCISES :

MAIN FOCUS :

MEALS :

SCHEDULE :

TO-DOS :

☐

☐

☐

☐

☐

☐

NOTES :

GOOD THINGS ABOUT TODAY :

WHAT I HOPE FOR TOMORROW :

DAY 41

"Believing in negative thoughts is the single great obstruction to success."
- Charles F. Glassman -

TODAY I'M EXCITED ABOUT :

EXERCISES :

MAIN FOCUS :

MEALS :

SCHEDULE :

TO-DOS :

- [ ]
- [ ]
- [ ]
- [ ]
- [ ]
- [ ]

NOTES :

GOOD THINGS ABOUT TODAY :

WHAT I HOPE FOR TOMORROW :

DAY 42

"We are the creators of our own experience. Remembering this and living our lives from this perspective empower us."
- Mike Robbins -

TODAY I'M EXCITED ABOUT :

EXERCISES :

MAIN FOCUS :

MEALS :

SCHEDULE :

TO-DOS :

☐

☐

☐

☐

☐

☐

NOTES :

GOOD THINGS ABOUT TODAY :

WHAT I HOPE FOR TOMORROW :

WEEKLY REFLECTION

DESCRIBE THIS PAST WEEK IN 3 WORDS :

	1	2	3	4	5	
Unhappy	1	2	3	4	5	Happy
Bored	1	2	3	4	5	Excited
Tired	1	2	3	4	5	Energetic
Stressed	1	2	3	4	5	Calm
Unhealthy	1	2	3	4	5	Healthy

Score _____ / 25

THIS WEEK'S HIGHS - GOOD / HAPPY / PROUD MOMENTS

THIS WEEK'S LOWS - FRUSTRATIONS / CHALLENGES / STRUGGLES

WEEKLY REFLECTION

WHAT I LEARNED THIS WEEK :

WHO & WHAT I'M THANKFUL FOR :

WHAT I'D LIKE TO IMPROVE / WHAT I HOPE FOR :

WEEKLY PLAN

MONDAY :

TUESDAY :

WEDNESDAY :

THURSDAY :

FRIDAY :

SATURDAY :

SUNDAY :

NOTES :

___ / ___
DATE

DAY 43

"Happiness is dependent on self-discipline. We are the biggest obstacles to our own happiness.
It is much easier to do battle with society and with others than to fight our own nature."
- Dennis Prager -

TODAY I'M EXCITED ABOUT :

EXERCISES :

MAIN FOCUS :

MEALS :

SCHEDULE :

TO-DOS :

- [ ]
- [ ]
- [ ]
- [ ]
- [ ]
- [ ]

NOTES :

GOOD THINGS ABOUT TODAY :

WHAT I HOPE FOR TOMORROW :

DAY 44

"Before you're about to give up on something because it's hard, remember that nothing worth having comes easy and every master was once a beginner."
- Mo Seetubtim -

TODAY I'M EXCITED ABOUT :

EXERCISES :

MAIN FOCUS :

MEALS :

SCHEDULE :

TO-DOS :

- ☐
- ☐
- ☐
- ☐
- ☐
- ☐

NOTES :

GOOD THINGS ABOUT TODAY :

WHAT I HOPE FOR TOMORROW :

/
DATE

DAY 45

"The very least you can do in your life is figure out what you hope for. And the most you can do is live inside that hope. Not admire it from a distance but live right under its roof."
- Barbara Kingsolver -

TODAY I'M EXCITED ABOUT :

EXERCISES :

MAIN FOCUS :

MEALS :

SCHEDULE :

TO-DOS :

- [ ]
- [ ]
- [ ]
- [ ]
- [ ]
- [ ]

NOTES :

GOOD THINGS ABOUT TODAY :

WHAT I HOPE FOR TOMORROW :

DAY 46

> "Happiness is not something you postpone for the future;
> it is something you design for the present."
> - Jim Rohn -

TODAY I'M EXCITED ABOUT :

EXERCISES :

MAIN FOCUS :

MEALS :

SCHEDULE :

TO-DOS :

- [ ]
- [ ]
- [ ]
- [ ]
- [ ]
- [ ]

NOTES :

GOOD THINGS ABOUT TODAY :

WHAT I HOPE FOR TOMORROW :

DATE

DAY 47

"Stop looking for reasons to be happy. Focus on the things you do have,
and the reasons you should be happy."
- Unknown -

TODAY I'M EXCITED ABOUT :

EXERCISES :

MAIN FOCUS :

MEALS :

SCHEDULE :

TO-DOS :

- [ ]
- [ ]
- [ ]
- [ ]
- [ ]
- [ ]

NOTES :

GOOD THINGS ABOUT TODAY :

WHAT I HOPE FOR TOMORROW :

DAY 48

"Every situation in life is temporary. So, when life is good, make sure you enjoy and receive it fully.
And when life is not good, remember that it will not last forever and better days are on the way."
- Jenni Young -

TODAY I'M EXCITED ABOUT :

EXERCISES :

MAIN FOCUS :

MEALS :

SCHEDULE :

TO-DOS :

☐

☐

☐

☐

☐

☐

NOTES :

GOOD THINGS ABOUT TODAY :

WHAT I HOPE FOR TOMORROW :

DAY 49

"Focus on the positive in your life, for what you focus on increases."
- Unknown -

TODAY I'M EXCITED ABOUT :

EXERCISES :

MAIN FOCUS :

MEALS :

SCHEDULE :

TO-DOS :

- [ ]
- [ ]
- [ ]
- [ ]
- [ ]
- [ ]

NOTES :

GOOD THINGS ABOUT TODAY :

WHAT I HOPE FOR TOMORROW :

WEEKLY REFLECTION

DESCRIBE THIS PAST WEEK IN 3 WORDS :

	1	2	3	4	5	
Unhappy	1	2	3	4	5	Happy
Bored	1	2	3	4	5	Excited
Tired	1	2	3	4	5	Energetic
Stressed	1	2	3	4	5	Calm
Unhealthy	1	2	3	4	5	Healthy

Score _____ / 25

THIS WEEK'S HIGHS - GOOD / HAPPY / PROUD MOMENTS

THIS WEEK'S LOWS - FRUSTRATIONS / CHALLENGES / STRUGGLES

WEEKLY REFLECTION

WHAT I LEARNED THIS WEEK :

WHO & WHAT I'M THANKFUL FOR :

WHAT I'D LIKE TO IMPROVE / WHAT I HOPE FOR :

WEEKLY PLAN

MONDAY :

TUESDAY :

WEDNESDAY :

THURSDAY :

FRIDAY :

SATURDAY :

SUNDAY :

NOTES :

DAY 50

"Remember that not getting what you want is sometimes a wonderful stroke of luck."
- Dalai Lama -

TODAY I'M EXCITED ABOUT :

EXERCISES :

MAIN FOCUS :

MEALS :

SCHEDULE :

TO-DOS :

- [ ]
- [ ]
- [ ]
- [ ]
- [ ]
- [ ]

NOTES :

GOOD THINGS ABOUT TODAY :

WHAT I HOPE FOR TOMORROW :

DAY 51

"The happiest of people don't necessarily have the best of everything;
they just make the most of everything that comes along their way."
- Karen S. Magee -

TODAY I'M EXCITED ABOUT :

EXERCISES :

MAIN FOCUS :

MEALS :

SCHEDULE :

TO-DOS :

☐
☐
☐
☐
☐
☐

NOTES :

GOOD THINGS ABOUT TODAY :

WHAT I HOPE FOR TOMORROW :

DAY 52

"Quit being so hard on yourself. We are what we are; we love what we love.
We don't need to justify it to anyone   not even to ourselves."
- Scott Lynch -

TODAY I'M EXCITED ABOUT :

EXERCISES :

MAIN FOCUS :

MEALS :

SCHEDULE :

TO-DOS :

☐

☐

☐

☐

☐

☐

NOTES :

GOOD THINGS ABOUT TODAY :

WHAT I HOPE FOR TOMORROW :

DAY 53

"Never let the things you want make you forget the things you have."
- Unknown -

TODAY I'M EXCITED ABOUT :

EXERCISES :

MAIN FOCUS :

MEALS :

SCHEDULE :

TO-DOS :

- [ ]
- [ ]
- [ ]
- [ ]
- [ ]
- [ ]

NOTES :

GOOD THINGS ABOUT TODAY :

WHAT I HOPE FOR TOMORROW :

DAY 54

"Once you learn to stop waiting for the world to give you what you want
and start giving it to yourself, you'll never be the same agian."
- Mo Seetubtim -

TODAY I'M EXCITED ABOUT :

EXERCISES :

MAIN FOCUS :

MEALS :

SCHEDULE :

TO-DOS :

- [ ]
- [ ]
- [ ]
- [ ]
- [ ]
- [ ]

NOTES :

GOOD THINGS ABOUT TODAY :

WHAT I HOPE FOR TOMORROW :

DAY 55

"It is not easy to find happiness in ourselves, and it is not possible to find it elsewhere."
- Agnes Repplier -

TODAY I'M EXCITED ABOUT :

EXERCISES :

MAIN FOCUS :

MEALS :

SCHEDULE :

TO-DOS :

- [ ]
- [ ]
- [ ]
- [ ]
- [ ]
- [ ]

NOTES :

GOOD THINGS ABOUT TODAY :

WHAT I HOPE FOR TOMORROW :

DAY 56

"Life is short, live it. Love is rare, grab it. Anger is bad, dump it.
Fear is awful, face it. Memories are sweet, cherish it."
- Unknown -

TODAY I'M EXCITED ABOUT :

EXERCISES :

MAIN FOCUS :

MEALS :

SCHEDULE :

TO-DOS :

☐

☐

☐

☐

☐

☐

NOTES :

GOOD THINGS ABOUT TODAY :

WHAT I HOPE FOR TOMORROW :

WEEKLY REFLECTION

DESCRIBE THIS PAST WEEK IN 3 WORDS :

	1	2	3	4	5	
Unhappy	1	2	3	4	5	Happy
Bored	1	2	3	4	5	Excited
Tired	1	2	3	4	5	Energetic
Stressed	1	2	3	4	5	Calm
Unhealthy	1	2	3	4	5	Healthy

Score _____ / 25

THIS WEEK'S HIGHS - GOOD / HAPPY / PROUD MOMENTS

THIS WEEK'S LOWS - FRUSTRATIONS / CHALLENGES / STRUGGLES

WHAT I LEARNED THIS WEEK :

WHO & WHAT I'M THANKFUL FOR :

WHAT I'D LIKE TO IMPROVE / WHAT I HOPE FOR :

WEEKLY PLAN

MONDAY :

TUESDAY :

WEDNESDAY :

THURSDAY :

FRIDAY :

SATURDAY :

SUNDAY :

NOTES :

DAY 57

"Comparison is the thief of joy."
- Theodore Roosevelt

TODAY I'M EXCITED ABOUT :

EXERCISES :

MAIN FOCUS :

MEALS :

SCHEDULE :

TO-DOS :

- [ ]
- [ ]
- [ ]
- [ ]
- [ ]
- [ ]

NOTES :

GOOD THINGS ABOUT TODAY :

WHAT I HOPE FOR TOMORROW :

DAY 58

> "The real value of setting goals is not the recognition or reward. It's the person we become by finding the discipline, courage, and commitment to achieve them."
> - Cat Smiley -

TODAY I'M EXCITED ABOUT :

EXERCISES :

MAIN FOCUS :

MEALS :

SCHEDULE :

TO-DOS :

☐

☐

☐

☐

☐

☐

NOTES :

GOOD THINGS ABOUT TODAY :

WHAT I HOPE FOR TOMORROW :

/
DATE

DAY 59

"Start by doing what's necessary; then do what's possible;
and suddenly you're doing the impossible."
- Francis of Assisi -

TODAY I'M EXCITED ABOUT :

EXERCISES :

MAIN FOCUS :

MEALS :

SCHEDULE :

TO-DOS :

- [ ]
- [ ]
- [ ]
- [ ]
- [ ]
- [ ]

NOTES :

GOOD THINGS ABOUT TODAY :

WHAT I HOPE FOR TOMORROW :

/
DATE

DAY 60

"One day you will wake up and there won't be any more time to do
the things you've always wanted. Do it now."
- Paulo Coelho -

TODAY I'M EXCITED ABOUT :

EXERCISES :

MAIN FOCUS :

MEALS :

SCHEDULE :

TO-DOS :

- [ ]
- [ ]
- [ ]
- [ ]
- [ ]
- [ ]

NOTES :

GOOD THINGS ABOUT TODAY :

WHAT I HOPE FOR TOMORROW :

DAY 61

"The more rules you have about how people have to be, how life has to be for
you to be happy, the less happy you're going to be."
- Tony Robbins -

TODAY I'M EXCITED ABOUT :

EXERCISES :

MAIN FOCUS :

MEALS :

SCHEDULE :

TO-DOS :

☐

☐

☐

☐

☐

☐

NOTES :

GOOD THINGS ABOUT TODAY :

WHAT I HOPE FOR TOMORROW :

DAY 62

"Talent without discipline is like an octopus on roller skates. There's plenty of movement, but you never know if it's going to be forward, backwards, or sideways."
- H. Jackson Brown Jr.

TODAY I'M EXCITED ABOUT :

EXERCISES :

MAIN FOCUS :

MEALS :

SCHEDULE :

TO-DOS :

☐

☐

☐

☐

☐

☐

NOTES :

GOOD THINGS ABOUT TODAY :

WHAT I HOPE FOR TOMORROW :

DAY 63

"To attract attractive people, you must be attractive. To attract powerful people, you must be powerful. To attract committed people, you must be committed. Instead of going to work on them, you go to work on yourself. If you become, you can attract."
- Jim Rohn -

TODAY I'M EXCITED ABOUT :

EXERCISES :

MAIN FOCUS :

MEALS :

SCHEDULE :

TO-DOS :

- [ ]
- [ ]
- [ ]
- [ ]
- [ ]
- [ ]

NOTES :

GOOD THINGS ABOUT TODAY :

WHAT I HOPE FOR TOMORROW :

WEEKLY REFLECTION

DESCRIBE THIS PAST WEEK IN 3 WORDS :

	1	2	3	4	5	
Unhappy	1	2	3	4	5	Happy
Bored	1	2	3	4	5	Excited
Tired	1	2	3	4	5	Energetic
Stressed	1	2	3	4	5	Calm
Unhealthy	1	2	3	4	5	Healthy

Score _____ / 25

THIS WEEK'S HIGHS - GOOD / HAPPY / PROUD MOMENTS

THIS WEEK'S LOWS - FRUSTRATIONS / CHALLENGES / STRUGGLES

WEEKLY REFLECTION

WHAT I LEARNED THIS WEEK :

WHO & WHAT I'M THANKFUL FOR :

WHAT I'D LIKE TO IMPROVE / WHAT I HOPE FOR :

WEEKLY PLAN

MONDAY :

TUESDAY :

WEDNESDAY :

THURSDAY :

FRIDAY :

SATURDAY :

SUNDAY :

NOTES :

DAY 64

"We should not judge people by their peak of excellence; but by the distance they
have traveled from the point where they started."
- Henry Ward Beecher -

TODAY I'M EXCITED ABOUT :

EXERCISES :

MAIN FOCUS :

MEALS :

SCHEDULE :

TO-DOS :

- [ ]
- [ ]
- [ ]
- [ ]
- [ ]
- [ ]

NOTES :

GOOD THINGS ABOUT TODAY :

WHAT I HOPE FOR TOMORROW :

DAY 65

"Be thankful for what you have; you'll end up having more. If you concentrate on what you don't have, you will never, ever have enough."
- Oprah Winfrey -

TODAY I'M EXCITED ABOUT :

EXERCISES :

MAIN FOCUS :

MEALS :

SCHEDULE :

TO-DOS :

- [ ]
- [ ]
- [ ]
- [ ]
- [ ]
- [ ]

NOTES :

GOOD THINGS ABOUT TODAY :

WHAT I HOPE FOR TOMORROW :

DAY 66

"The journey of a thousand miles begins with one step."
- Lao Tzu -

TODAY I'M EXCITED ABOUT :

EXERCISES :

MAIN FOCUS :

MEALS :

SCHEDULE :

TO-DOS :

☐

☐

☐

☐

☐

☐

NOTES :

GOOD THINGS ABOUT TODAY :

WHAT I HOPE FOR TOMORROW :

DAY 67

"It is never too late to be what you might have been."
- George Eliot -

TODAY I'M EXCITED ABOUT :

EXERCISES :

MAIN FOCUS :

MEALS :

SCHEDULE :

TO-DOS :

☐ ....

☐ ....

☐ ....

☐ ....

☐ ....

☐ ....

NOTES :

GOOD THINGS ABOUT TODAY :

WHAT I HOPE FOR TOMORROW :

DAY 68

"Ten years from now, make sure you can say that you chose your life,
you didn't settle for it."
- Mandy Hale -

TODAY I'M EXCITED ABOUT :

EXERCISES :

MAIN FOCUS :

MEALS :

SCHEDULE :

TO-DOS :

- [ ]
- [ ]
- [ ]
- [ ]
- [ ]
- [ ]

NOTES :

GOOD THINGS ABOUT TODAY :

WHAT I HOPE FOR TOMORROW :

DAY 69

"Once we accept our limits, we go beyond them."
- Albert Einstein -

TODAY I'M EXCITED ABOUT :

EXERCISES :

MAIN FOCUS :

MEALS :

SCHEDULE :

TO-DOS :

☐
☐
☐
☐
☐
☐

NOTES :

GOOD THINGS ABOUT TODAY :

WHAT I HOPE FOR TOMORROW :

DAY 70

"To succeed, you need to find something to hold on to, something to motivate you,
something to inspire you."
- Tony Dorsett -

TODAY I'M EXCITED ABOUT :

EXERCISES :

MAIN FOCUS :

MEALS :

SCHEDULE :

TO-DOS :

- [ ]
- [ ]
- [ ]
- [ ]
- [ ]
- [ ]

NOTES :

GOOD THINGS ABOUT TODAY :

WHAT I HOPE FOR TOMORROW :

WEEKLY REFLECTION

DESCRIBE THIS PAST WEEK IN 3 WORDS :

	1	2	3	4	5	
Unhappy	1	2	3	4	5	Happy
Bored	1	2	3	4	5	Excited
Tired	1	2	3	4	5	Energetic
Stressed	1	2	3	4	5	Calm
Unhealthy	1	2	3	4	5	Healthy

Score _____ / 25

THIS WEEK'S HIGHS - GOOD / HAPPY / PROUD MOMENTS

THIS WEEK'S LOWS - FRUSTRATIONS / CHALLENGES / STRUGGLES

WEEKLY REFLECTION

WHAT I LEARNED THIS WEEK :

WHO & WHAT I'M THANKFUL FOR :

WHAT I'D LIKE TO IMPROVE / WHAT I HOPE FOR :

WEEKLY PLAN

MONDAY :

TUESDAY :

WEDNESDAY :

THURSDAY :

FRIDAY :

SATURDAY :

SUNDAY :

NOTES :

DAY 71

"True belonging can only happen when we present our authentic, imperfect selves to the world. Our sense of belonging can never be greater than our level of self-acceptance."
- Brene Brown -

TODAY I'M EXCITED ABOUT :

EXERCISES :

MAIN FOCUS :

MEALS :

SCHEDULE :

TO-DOS :

☐

☐

☐

☐

☐

☐

NOTES :

GOOD THINGS ABOUT TODAY :

WHAT I HOPE FOR TOMORROW :

DAY 72

"Only those who risk going too far can possibly find out how far one can go."
- T. S. Eliot -

TODAY I'M EXCITED ABOUT :

EXERCISES :

MAIN FOCUS :

MEALS :

SCHEDULE :

TO-DOS :

☐
☐
☐
☐
☐
☐

NOTES :

GOOD THINGS ABOUT TODAY :

WHAT I HOPE FOR TOMORROW :

DAY 73

"In the end, just three things matter: How well we have lived.
How well we have loved. How well we have learned to let go."
- Jack Kornfield -

TODAY I'M EXCITED ABOUT :

EXERCISES :

MAIN FOCUS :

MEALS :

SCHEDULE :

TO-DOS :

☐

☐

☐

☐

☐

☐

NOTES :

GOOD THINGS ABOUT TODAY :

WHAT I HOPE FOR TOMORROW :

_____ /
DATE

DAY 74

"Affirmations are our mental vitamins, providing the supplementary positive thoughts
we need to balance the barrage of negative events and thoughts we expeirence daily."
- Tia Walker -

TODAY I'M EXCITED ABOUT :

EXERCISES :

MAIN FOCUS :

MEALS :

SCHEDULE :

TO-DOS :

☐

☐

☐

☐

☐

☐

NOTES :

GOOD THINGS ABOUT TODAY :

WHAT I HOPE FOR TOMORROW :

DAY 75

"If you don't like something, change it. If you can't change it, change your attitude.
Don't complain."
- Maya Angelou -

TODAY I'M EXCITED ABOUT :

EXERCISES :

MAIN FOCUS :

MEALS :

SCHEDULE :

TO-DOS :

- [ ]
- [ ]
- [ ]
- [ ]
- [ ]
- [ ]

NOTES :

GOOD THINGS ABOUT TODAY :

WHAT I HOPE FOR TOMORROW :

DAY 76

"Retraining the mind to think positive thoughts is a tremendous valuable
endeavor that can change your life."
- Lance Dale -

TODAY I'M EXCITED ABOUT :

EXERCISES :

MAIN FOCUS :

MEALS :

SCHEDULE :

TO-DOS :

☐

☐

☐

☐

☐

☐

NOTES :

GOOD THINGS ABOUT TODAY :

WHAT I HOPE FOR TOMORROW :

DAY 77

"Let go off your attachment to being right, and suddenly your mind is more oepn. You're able to benefit from the unique viewpoints of others without being crippled by your own judgement."
- Ralph Marston -

TODAY I'M EXCITED ABOUT :

EXERCISES :

MAIN FOCUS :

MEALS :

SCHEDULE :

TO-DOS :

- [ ]
- [ ]
- [ ]
- [ ]
- [ ]
- [ ]

NOTES :

GOOD THINGS ABOUT TODAY :

WHAT I HOPE FOR TOMORROW :

WEEKLY REFLECTION

DESCRIBE THIS PAST WEEK IN 3 WORDS :

Unhappy	1	2	3	4	5	Happy
Bored	1	2	3	4	5	Excited
Tired	1	2	3	4	5	Energetic
Stressed	1	2	3	4	5	Calm
Unhealthy	1	2	3	4	5	Healthy

Score _____ / 25

THIS WEEK'S HIGHS - GOOD / HAPPY / PROUD MOMENTS

THIS WEEK'S LOWS - FRUSTRATIONS / CHALLENGES / STRUGGLES

WEEKLY REFLECTION

WHAT I LEARNED THIS WEEK :

WHO & WHAT I'M THANKFUL FOR :

WHAT I'D LIKE TO IMPROVE / WHAT I HOPE FOR :

WEEKLY PLAN

MONDAY :

TUESDAY :

WEDNESDAY :

THURSDAY :

FRIDAY :

SATURDAY :

SUNDAY :

NOTES :

DAY 78

"I believe we create our own lives. And we create it by our thinking, feeling patterns in
our belief system. I think we're all born with this huge canvas in front of us and
the paintbrushes and the paint, and we choose what to put on this canvas."
- Louise L. Hay -

TODAY I'M EXCITED ABOUT :

EXERCISES :

MAIN FOCUS :

MEALS :

SCHEDULE :

TO-DOS :

- [ ]
- [ ]
- [ ]
- [ ]
- [ ]
- [ ]

NOTES :

GOOD THINGS ABOUT TODAY :

WHAT I HOPE FOR TOMORROW :

DAY 79

"Once we discover how to appreciate the timeless values in our daily experiences,
we can enjoy the best things in life."
- Jerome K. Jerome -

TODAY I'M EXCITED ABOUT :

EXERCISES :

MAIN FOCUS :

MEALS :

SCHEDULE :

TO-DOS :

- [ ]
- [ ]
- [ ]
- [ ]
- [ ]
- [ ]

NOTES :

GOOD THINGS ABOUT TODAY :

WHAT I HOPE FOR TOMORROW :

/
DATE

DAY 80

"Focus on what makes you happy. Do what gives meaning to your life."
- Barry Schwartz -

TODAY I'M EXCITED ABOUT :

EXERCISES :

MAIN FOCUS :

MEALS :

SCHEDULE :

TO-DOS :

- [ ]
- [ ]
- [ ]
- [ ]
- [ ]
- [ ]

NOTES :

GOOD THINGS ABOUT TODAY :

WHAT I HOPE FOR TOMORROW :

DAY 81

"What is the difference between an obstacle and an opportunity? Our attitude towards it. Every opportunity has a difficulty, and every difficulty has an opportunity."
- J. Sidlow Baxter -

TODAY I'M EXCITED ABOUT :

EXERCISES :

MAIN FOCUS :

MEALS :

SCHEDULE :

TO-DOS :

☐

☐

☐

☐

☐

☐

NOTES :

GOOD THINGS ABOUT TODAY :

WHAT I HOPE FOR TOMORROW :

/
DATE

DAY 82

"Trust in the perfection of your life and let yourself be fully where you are in the moment.
Trust that you are exactly where you are supposed to be. Know that what you have to look
forward to is greater than what you are leaving behind."
- Sonya Derian -

TODAY I'M EXCITED ABOUT :

EXERCISES :

MAIN FOCUS :

MEALS :

SCHEDULE :

TO-DOS :

- [ ]
- [ ]
- [ ]
- [ ]
- [ ]
- [ ]

NOTES :

GOOD THINGS ABOUT TODAY :

WHAT I HOPE FOR TOMORROW :

/
DATE

DAY 83

"Do the things that inspire us so we can inspire other people to do the things that inspire them. But we can't find that unless we know what we're looking for. We have to do our work on ourselves - be intentional about making those discoveries."
Scott Dinsmore -

TODAY I'M EXCITED ABOUT :

EXERCISES :

MAIN FOCUS :

MEALS :

SCHEDULE :

TO-DOS :

- [ ]
- [ ]
- [ ]
- [ ]
- [ ]
- [ ]

NOTES :

GOOD THINGS ABOUT TODAY :

WHAT I HOPE FOR TOMORROW :

DAY 84

"To be yourself in a world that is constantly trying to make you
something else is the greatest accomplishment."
- Ralph Waldo Emerson -

TODAY I'M EXCITED ABOUT :

EXERCISES :

MAIN FOCUS :

MEALS :

SCHEDULE :

TO-DOS :

☐

☐

☐

☐

☐

☐

NOTES :

GOOD THINGS ABOUT TODAY :

WHAT I HOPE FOR TOMORROW :

WEEKLY REFLECTION

DESCRIBE THIS PAST WEEK IN 3 WORDS :

	1	2	3	4	5	
Unhappy	1	2	3	4	5	Happy
Bored	1	2	3	4	5	Excited
Tired	1	2	3	4	5	Energetic
Stressed	1	2	3	4	5	Calm
Unhealthy	1	2	3	4	5	Healthy

Score _____ / 25

THIS WEEK'S HIGHS - GOOD / HAPPY / PROUD MOMENTS

THIS WEEK'S LOWS - FRUSTRATIONS / CHALLENGES / STRUGGLES

WEEKLY REFLECTION

WHAT I LEARNED THIS WEEK :

WHO & WHAT I'M THANKFUL FOR :

WHAT I'D LIKE TO IMPROVE / WHAT I HOPE FOR :

WEEKLY PLAN

MONDAY :

TUESDAY :

WEDNESDAY :

THURSDAY :

FRIDAY :

SATURDAY :

SUNDAY :

NOTES :

DAY 85

"Ego says, 'Once everything falls into place, I'll feel peace.',
Spirit says, 'Find your peace, and then everything will fall into place.'"
- Marianne Williamson -

TODAY I'M EXCITED ABOUT :

EXERCISES :

MAIN FOCUS :

MEALS :

SCHEDULE :

TO-DOS :

☐

☐

☐

☐

☐

☐

NOTES :

GOOD THINGS ABOUT TODAY :

WHAT I HOPE FOR TOMORROW :

DAY 86

"The secret of success is learning how to use pain and pleasure instead of having pain and pleasure use you. If you do that, you're in control of your life. If you don't life controls you."
- Tony Robbins -

TODAY I'M EXCITED ABOUT :

EXERCISES :

MAIN FOCUS :

MEALS :

SCHEDULE :

TO-DOS :

☐

☐

☐

☐

☐

☐

NOTES :

GOOD THINGS ABOUT TODAY :

WHAT I HOPE FOR TOMORROW :

DATE

DAY 87

"One's destination is never a place, but a new way of seeing things."
- Henry Miller -

TODAY I'M EXCITED ABOUT :

EXERCISES :

MAIN FOCUS :

MEALS :

SCHEDULE :

TO-DOS :

- [ ]
- [ ]
- [ ]
- [ ]
- [ ]
- [ ]

NOTES :

GOOD THINGS ABOUT TODAY :

WHAT I HOPE FOR TOMORROW :

DAY 88

"The great thing in the world is not so much where we stand, as in what direction we are moving."
- Oliver Wendell Holmes, Sr.-

TODAY I'M EXCITED ABOUT :

EXERCISES :

MAIN FOCUS :

MEALS :

SCHEDULE :

TO-DOS :

- [ ]
- [ ]
- [ ]
- [ ]
- [ ]
- [ ]

NOTES :

GOOD THINGS ABOUT TODAY :

WHAT I HOPE FOR TOMORROW :

DAY 89

"At least once a year, go someplace you've never been before
and do something you've never done before."
- Mo Seetubtim -

TODAY I'M EXCITED ABOUT :

EXERCISES :

MAIN FOCUS :

MEALS :

SCHEDULE :

TO-DOS :

- [ ]
- [ ]
- [ ]
- [ ]
- [ ]
- [ ]

NOTES :

GOOD THINGS ABOUT TODAY :

WHAT I HOPE FOR TOMORROW :

DAY 90

"The reason we struggle with insecurity is because we compare
our behind-the-scenes with everyone else's highlight reel."
- Steven Furtick -

TODAY I'M EXCITED ABOUT :

EXERCISES :

MAIN FOCUS :

MEALS :

SCHEDULE :

TO-DOS :

☐

☐

☐

☐

☐

☐

NOTES :

GOOD THINGS ABOUT TODAY :

WHAT I HOPE FOR TOMORROW :

DAY 91

> "Great things are not done by impulse, but by a series of
> small things brought together."
> - Vicent Van Gogh -

TODAY I'M EXCITED ABOUT :

EXERCISES :

MAIN FOCUS :

MEALS :

SCHEDULE :

TO-DOS :

- [ ]
- [ ]
- [ ]
- [ ]
- [ ]
- [ ]

NOTES :

GOOD THINGS ABOUT TODAY :

WHAT I HOPE FOR TOMORROW :

WEEKLY REFLECTION

DESCRIBE THIS PAST WEEK IN 3 WORDS :

Unhappy	1	2	3	4	5	Happy
Bored	1	2	3	4	5	Excited
Tired	1	2	3	4	5	Energetic
Stressed	1	2	3	4	5	Calm
Unhealthy	1	2	3	4	5	Healthy

Score _____ / 25

THIS WEEK'S HIGHS - GOOD / HAPPY / PROUD MOMENTS

THIS WEEK'S LOWS - FRUSTRATIONS / CHALLENGES / STRUGGLES

WEEKLY REFLECTION

WHAT I LEARNED THIS WEEK :

WHO & WHAT I'M THANKFUL FOR :

WHAT I'D LIKE TO IMPROVE / WHAT I HOPE FOR :

WEEKLY PLAN

MONDAY :

TUESDAY :

WEDNESDAY :

THURSDAY :

FRIDAY :

SATURDAY :

SUNDAY :

NOTES :

DAY 92

"You can run, run, run away from a lot of things in life, but you can't run away from yourself.
And the key to happiness is to understand and accept who you are."
- Dale Archer -

TODAY I'M EXCITED ABOUT :

EXERCISES :

MAIN FOCUS :

MEALS :

SCHEDULE :

TO-DOS :

☐

☐

☐

☐

☐

☐

NOTES :

GOOD THINGS ABOUT TODAY :

WHAT I HOPE FOR TOMORROW :

_____ / _____
DATE

DAY 93

"Most people ask for happiness on condition.
Happiness can only be felt if you don't set any condition."
- Arthur Rubinstein -

TODAY I'M EXCITED ABOUT :

EXERCISES :

MAIN FOCUS :

MEALS :

SCHEDULE :

TO-DOS :

☐

☐

☐

☐

☐

☐

NOTES :

GOOD THINGS ABOUT TODAY :

WHAT I HOPE FOR TOMORROW :

DAY 94

"If you change the way you look at things, the things you look at change."
- Wayne Dyer -

TODAY I'M EXCITED ABOUT :

EXERCISES :

MAIN FOCUS :

MEALS :

SCHEDULE :

TO-DOS :

☐

☐

☐

☐

☐

☐

NOTES :

GOOD THINGS ABOUT TODAY :

WHAT I HOPE FOR TOMORROW :

DAY 95

"Remember that the end of something good is the beginning of something better."
- Mo Seetubtim -

TODAY I'M EXCITED ABOUT :

EXERCISES :

MAIN FOCUS :

MEALS :

SCHEDULE :

TO-DOS :

- [ ]
- [ ]
- [ ]
- [ ]
- [ ]
- [ ]

NOTES :

GOOD THINGS ABOUT TODAY :

WHAT I HOPE FOR TOMORROW :

DATE

DAY 96

"Don't let fear or insecurity stop you from trying new things. Believe in yourself.
Do what you love. And most importantly, be kind to others even if you don't like them."
- Stacy London -

TODAY I'M EXCITED ABOUT :

EXERCISES :

MAIN FOCUS :

MEALS :

SCHEDULE :

TO-DOS :

- [ ]
- [ ]
- [ ]
- [ ]
- [ ]
- [ ]

NOTES :

GOOD THINGS ABOUT TODAY :

WHAT I HOPE FOR TOMORROW :

DAY 97

"You are confined only by the walls you build yourself".
- Andrew Murphy -

TODAY I'M EXCITED ABOUT :

EXERCISES :

MAIN FOCUS :

MEALS :

SCHEDULE :

TO-DOS :

☐

☐

☐

☐

☐

☐

NOTES :

GOOD THINGS ABOUT TODAY :

WHAT I HOPE FOR TOMORROW :

DAY 98

"Your comfort zone keeps expanding every time you get out of your comfort zone."
- Mo Seetubtim -

TODAY I'M EXCITED ABOUT :

EXERCISES :

MAIN FOCUS :

MEALS :

SCHEDULE :

TO-DOS :

- [ ]
- [ ]
- [ ]
- [ ]
- [ ]
- [ ]

NOTES :

GOOD THINGS ABOUT TODAY :

WHAT I HOPE FOR TOMORROW :

WEEKLY REFLECTION

DESCRIBE THIS PAST WEEK IN 3 WORDS :

	1	2	3	4	5	
Unhappy	1	2	3	4	5	Happy
Bored	1	2	3	4	5	Excited
Tired	1	2	3	4	5	Energetic
Stressed	1	2	3	4	5	Calm
Unhealthy	1	2	3	4	5	Healthy

Score _____ / 25

THIS WEEK'S HIGHS - GOOD / HAPPY / PROUD MOMENTS

THIS WEEK'S LOWS - FRUSTRATIONS / CHALLENGES / STRUGGLES

WEEKLY REFLECTION

WHAT I LEARNED THIS WEEK :

WHO & WHAT I'M THANKFUL FOR :

WHAT I'D LIKE TO IMPROVE / WHAT I HOPE FOR :

WEEKLY PLAN

MONDAY :

TUESDAY :

WEDNESDAY :

THURSDAY :

FRIDAY :

SATURDAY :

SUNDAY :

NOTES :

DAY 99

"Your life consists of the stories you tell yourself about what happened to yourself.
So do your best to choose your reactions."
- Mo Seetubtim -

TODAY I'M EXCITED ABOUT :

EXERCISES :

MAIN FOCUS :

MEALS :

SCHEDULE :

TO-DOS :

☐

☐

☐

☐

☐

☐

NOTES :

GOOD THINGS ABOUT TODAY :

WHAT I HOPE FOR TOMORROW :

DAY 100

"Life is a journey and if you fall in love with the journey, you will be in love forever."
- Peter Hagerty -

TODAY I'M EXCITED ABOUT :

EXERCISES :

MAIN FOCUS :

MEALS :

SCHEDULE :

TO-DOS :

- [ ]
- [ ]
- [ ]
- [ ]
- [ ]
- [ ]

NOTES :

GOOD THINGS ABOUT TODAY :

WHAT I HOPE FOR TOMORROW :

You find peace not by rearranging the circumstances of your life, but by realizing who you are at the deepest level.

- Eckhart Tolle -

FILL OUT YOUR SCORES FROM THE PAST 100 DAYS.

How you feel / Week	Unhappy - Happy	Bored - Excited	Tired - Energetic	Stressed - Calm	Unhealthy - Healthy	Total weekly
Week 1						
Week 2						
Week 4						
Week 4						
Week 5						
Week 6						
Week 7						
Week 8						
Week 9						
Week 10						
Week 11						
Week 12						
Week 13						
Week 14						
Total Scores						

NOTES :

....

....

....

....

100-DAY REVIEW

1. Describe the past 100 days in 3 words

....

....

2. What was your most common state of mind (e.g. happy, tired, or stressed) ?

....

....

3. What were your happiest moments?

....

....

....

....

....

....

....

....

....

....

....

....

....

4. What little things did you most enjoy doing on a daily basis?

5. What new skills did you learn?

6. What personal qualities or habits did you develop, cultivate, or strengthen?

7. What new things did you discover about yourself?

8. What did you do that got you out of your comfort zone?

9. Did any negative events happen? How did you overcome them?

10. What and who are you most thankful for?